This Ladybird book
belongs to

....

To my beloved son, Rian,
and his primary bestie, Ryan Skelly.
Even as four-year-olds, they knew.
L. H. A. MBE

To my husband, Curtly.
Thank you for the support, the encouragement,
the laughter and the company through
the long working weekends!

To my son, Kamsi.
You arrived in the nick of time, thanks for being here!
O. I.

LADYBIRD BOOKS

UK | USA | Canada | Ireland | Australia
India | New Zealand | South Africa

Ladybird Books is part of the Penguin Random House group of companies
whose addresses can be found at global.penguinrandomhouse.com.
www.penguin.co.uk   www.puffin.co.uk   www.ladybird.co.uk

Penguin
Random House
UK

First published 2021
001
Written by Laura Henry-Allain MBE
Illustrated by Onyinye Iwu
Copyright © Ladybird Books Ltd, 2021
Printed in China
The authorized representative in the EEA is Penguin Random House Ireland,
Morrison Chambers, 32 Nassau Street, Dublin D02 YH68
A CIP catalogue record for this book is available from the British Library
ISBN: 978–0–241–51273–9

All correspondence to:
Ladybird Books, Penguin Random House Children's
One Embassy Gardens, 8 Viaduct Gardens
London SW11 7BW

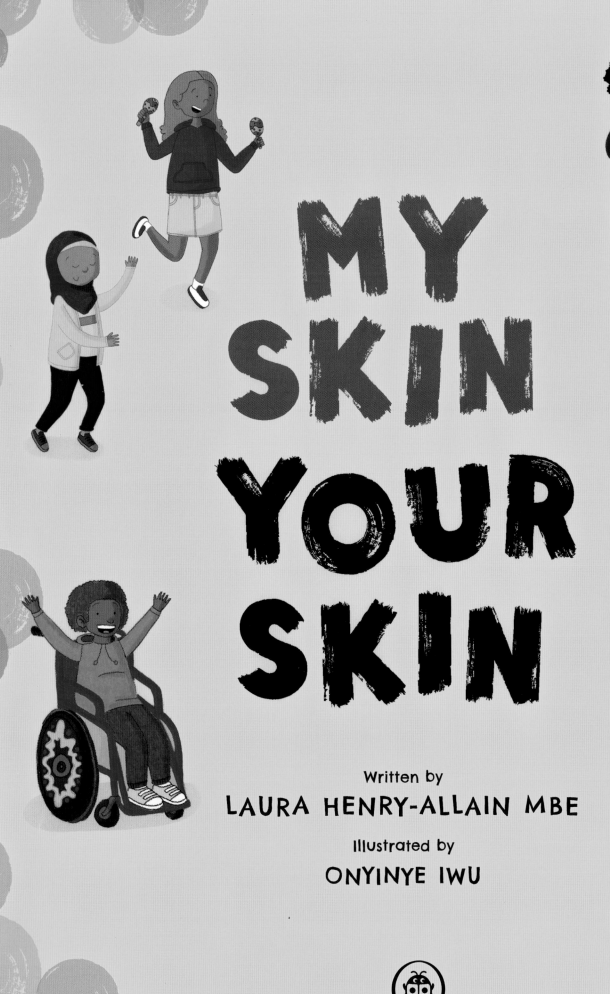

MY SKIN YOUR SKIN

Written by
LAURA HENRY-ALLAIN MBE

Illustrated by
ONYINYE IWU

We are all different.

Our skin colours are different.
Our eye colours are different.

We could be small
or big, tall or short.

We could have
one arm or two.

Think about all the people that you know, such as your family,
friends and teachers. How are they different from one another?

Our differences make us amazing!

It's fun to discuss and celebrate our differences with our friends.

We could be Muslim or Buddhist or Christian or Jewish or Hindu, or we could have no religion at all.

We could live with a mum and dad, with a dad, two mums, a grandparent or in a foster family.

We both have brown hair, but mine is short and straight, and yours is curly.

Your parents were both born in England, but my mummy comes from St Lucia, and my daddy comes from Scotland.

Be **proud** of what makes you different. This will help others to share their differences and help them be proud, too.

What makes you amazing?

People who share the same skin colour are often said to be of the same race.
People of the same race sometimes have similarly shaped lips or eyes, too.

The word **race** is just a way of grouping people together – it doesn't mean that everybody in that group is the same, even if their skin is a similar colour or their lips or eyes have similar shapes.

You should be proud of your skin colour, your lips, your hair and every part of you.

You are amazing.

Our **culture** is the way we do things together. It is different to our race.
Different cultures make the world bigger, better and more exciting.

The world is full of people of different races.
This is what makes the world so fun and interesting!

Once we know that there are different races, we can
begin to talk about them. Some people feel uncomfortable
talking about race, but **we** do not need to be.

My friend is Black.

My mummy is Chinese,
and my daddy is Ghanaian.

My cousin is white.

What colour is your skin? Do you know lots of people
whose race is different to yours, or a few, or none?

What is racism?

- ▶ Racism started a long time ago when white people wanted to have more control over other people who were not white.

- ▶ Racism is about systems in society that are deeply embedded and are about power.

- ▶ Racism is treating somebody in a nasty way because of their race.

- ▶ Racism isn't always about calling people names; it is also about the way that things are done to stop people who are not white from being equal.

- ▶ An example of racism is when white people think they are better than people from other races, and treat those who are, for example, Black, of South Asian heritage or of East and South East Asian heritage, in a nasty way.

- ▶ Another example of racism is when an organisation, like a school, only has white people in charge and never anybody who is Black or of South Asian, East or South East Asian heritage and says it's because they couldn't find anybody else who was good enough for the job.

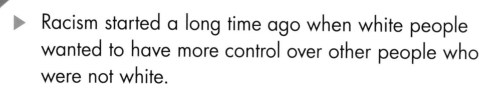

Racism is WRONG.

It is NEVER OK to be racist.

It is **NOT OK** for someone to treat another person differently because of their race.

It is **NOT OK** for someone to think they are better than someone else because of their race.

If you hear another child being racist, you should use your loud voice to tell them:

That is wrong!

If you feel scared, you could tell a parent, a teacher or an adult who is special to you and makes you feel safe. Tell them, "I heard someone being racist". They can support you.

People can be racist anywhere –

at home

or at school,

a place of worship

or in shops.

They can be racist in what they say or how they act.

Some people are more racist to particular groups. For example, racism specifically towards Black people is called anti-Blackness.

Being racist is NEVER OK.

Leaving someone out of a game because of their race . . .

is wrong.

Being mean about someone's hair type . . .

is wrong.

Saying that a Black doll is ugly . . .

is wrong.

Calling someone a name based on their race . . .

is wrong.

People can be **anything** they want to be.

Race has **nothing** to do with what someone can achieve.

Anyone can be a . . .

TV presenter

teacher

scientist

lawyer

builder

author

doctor

classical
musician

ballet
dancer

artist

astronaut

chef

pilot

firefighter

vet

mechanic

How might a person feel when someone has been racist to them?
They might feel . . .

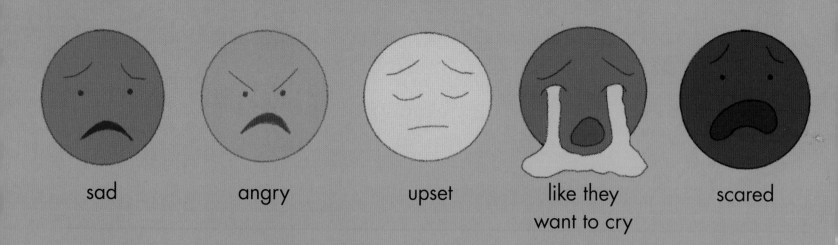

sad

angry

upset

like they
want to cry

scared

It is OK to have these feelings when someone is racist to you.
If this happens, you should always tell an adult that you trust.

Has anyone ever been mean
to you about your race?

How did it make you feel?

Have you ever been mean to
someone about their race?

How do you think it
made them feel?

Has anyone ever been mean to
your friend because of their race?

How do you think that
made them feel?

If someone is racist to you, it is **not** your fault.

Remember, every one of us is special, and no one should be treated badly because of the colour of their skin.

We should celebrate our differences!

We are **all** born with beautiful skin.

We are not born racist.

Racism often happens when a person copies someone else's racist words or actions.

It is wrong.

This is how racism continues.

It is wrong.

We can stop racism.

That is right.

You may hear someone being racist about you or being racist to you.

You may see someone being racist to someone else.

You must tell an adult. This could be a parent, teacher or any grown-up who is special to you.

It is NEVER OK for someone to be racist to you or anyone else.

It is NEVER OK for you to be racist to other people.

Racism is bullying.

Racism makes others invisible.

Racism is like hitting someone.

Racism is not right!

Sadly, racism is a problem all over the world.

It is a big and difficult problem.

It has been around for years and years.

You can't dismantle racism by yourself.
It would take everyone in the world to stop being racist.

But if you learn to recognize racism and speak out when you see it, you are already helping to stop it. This is called being **anti-racist**.

It is important to be kind and to respect others. But being anti-racist is about much more than that. It is about using our voices to speak up when we see someone being racist. It is about reading books about people from other races. It is about making friends with others who are from many different races.

By taking time to get to know our new friends, we can learn more about their lives. This will help us to understand that one race is not better than another – it is just different.

Aren't we lucky to know so many people who are different to us?

There's so much we can do to stop racism from spreading.

Above all, we should **celebrate** our different races and cultures.
When we do this . . .

. . . we learn new ideas.

. . . we make new friends.

. . . we celebrate
new festivals.

. . . we eat new foods.

. . . we learn new words.

. . . we discover that people from different races and cultures created objects and ideas that changed the way we do things every day.

There is so much to celebrate in this wonderful world.

Glossary

anti-Blackness
a type of racism that only targets Black people

anti-racist
taking positive actions to help stop racism

bullying
repeatedly hurting someone on purpose, either physically or emotionally or both

culture
the way a group of people lives, including their customs and beliefs

race
a term that groups humans according to their skin colour and features

racism
feeling or behaving badly towards someone because of their race, or believing that white people are better than people of other races

racist
behaving badly towards someone else because of their race, or believing that one race is better than another

Questions

Tell me about your skin colour.

What makes your family unique?

Which special festivals do you and your family celebrate?

A note for adults reading this book

This book is a starting point for discussing race, racism and empowerment. These conversations are vital. Being anti-racist is essential.

Here are some things you could do to help support young children to tackle racism:

- Make a list of behaviours that are unacceptable. This could be added to a list of family values or school values.

- Reflect on your own biases and past behaviour. We need to reflect on the past in order to move forward.

- Help your child to develop good self-esteem. This will not stop racism, but it will help them be proud of their identity. Try using daily affirmation cards, with messages like "Your skin is beautiful" and "You are special".

- Have a range of toys, including dolls and action figures of different races and cultures. Observe your child as they play. Are they including Black and Asian dolls in their play, for example? If not, pick one up and join in.

- Discuss and share, where appropriate, injustices that have happened in the world.

- Never dismiss your child's experiences of racism, whether they are on the receiving end or a witness. Telling them not to worry or to ignore bullies is not helpful. Help them understand that it is not their fault, and encourage them to explore their feelings using words.

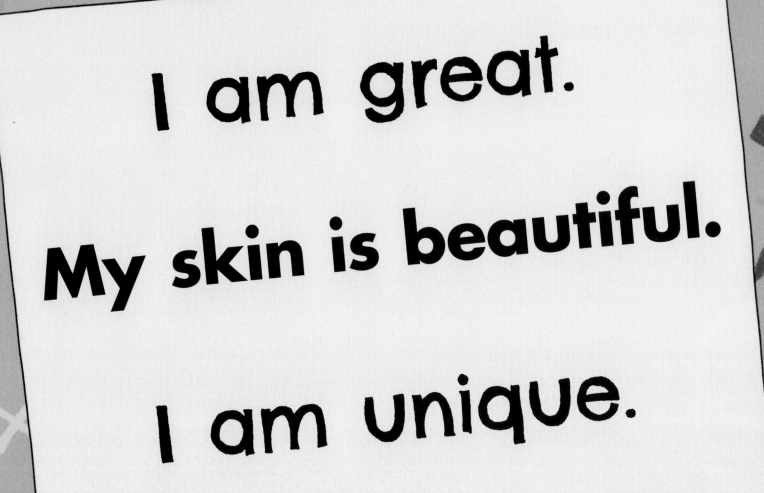

I am great.

My skin is beautiful.

I am unique.

The author would like to thank Liz Pemberton,
aka The Black Nursery Manager, and
Dr Eunice Lumsden, Head of Early Years and
Associate Professor at the University of Northampton.

Laura Henry-Allain MBE is an international award-winning early education specialist, writer and children's media creator.

Onyinye Iwu is a Nigerian illustrator and author. She was born in Italy, where she spent her childhood, and then moved to the UK. Onyinye enjoys reading books and drawing patterns.